Poetry Zooms In

Poetry Zooms In

On the Sacred in Persons and World

CARROLL E. ARKEMA

RESOURCE *Publications* · Eugene, Oregon

POETRY ZOOMS IN
On the Sacred in Persons and World

Resource Publications
An Imprint of Wipf and Stock Publishers
199 W. 8th Ave., Suite 3
Eugene, OR 97401

www.wipfandstock.com

PAPERBACK ISBN: 978-1-6667-3543-7
HARDCOVER ISBN: 978-1-6667-9250-8
EBOOK ISBN: 978-1-6667-9251-5

01/13/22

"Covid Confronts Me" is reprinted from the Journal of Pastoral Care and Counseling, Volume 75, Issue 2 (June) 2021, pp, 139–39, with kind permission from Green Open Access: SAGE's Archiving and Sharing Policy.

Scripture quotations noted The Holy Bible (NRSV) are taken from the New Revised Standard Version Bible, copyright 1989, Division of Christian Education of the National Council of the Churches of Christ in the United States of America. Used by permission. All rights reserved.

Scripture taken from the New King James Version®. Copyright © 1982 by Thomas Nelson. Used by permission. All rights reserved.

This book is dedicated to

Mairead Stack

My Life Partner
for over twenty-five years,
in gratitude for her unfailing love
and "Her Smile"
(see the poem inside).

Contents

Author's Preface

As I COLLECTED MY poems for this book, my first thought for a title was "Musings Sacred and Mundane," which captures my underlying orientation as I write. Poets have often been called "Muses," or they're thought of as listening to their Muse. The New Random House Dictionary[1] defines the verb "to muse" as: "to reflect in silence and usually dreamily," or "to consider or say reflectively." It lists some synonyms as: "to meditate, ponder, ruminate." All these sound accurate to me. I thought of the words "Sacred and Mundane" because I am usually—at some level of awareness—musing about the presence of the Sacred, the Holy, in what I'm writing about—specifically about It being present and seen in the mundane world. When I'm writing, I muse about "the Sacred" implicitly if not explicitly.

Then one day—seemingly out of the blue, I found myself reciting silently the words from Psalm nineteen, verse two: "Day unto day utters speech, and night unto night reveals knowledge."[2] I wondered if I could use some of that as a title—specifically, "Day Unto Day Utters Speech." Day after day does indeed tell the wonders of this world, but I found this verse to be an even more compelling title (shortened to that first part), because it embraces the reality and importance of night, or darkness, as well as daylight. The verse asserts that there is much to be learned from literal and metaphorical darkness as well as light.

1. *The Random House Dictionary.*
2. *The Holy Bible NKJV*, Psalm 19:2.

Author's Preface

Some of my poems express my belief and experience that there simply is a dark part of every human being, and that these innate dark impulses will express themselves destructively in hurtful behavior or ill health if they aren't identified, acknowledged, and dealt with constructively. The way to prevent their destructive expressions or manifestations is to acknowledge their presence in oneself, which gives oneself just enough distance from the darkness to manage it and express it constructively.

Darkness is a part of the whole of a person, and it can be managed and even transformed if it is acknowledged. Which is not easy to do: I repeat, acknowledging the darkness in oneself is not easy to do. One's discomfort with accepting darkness inside oneself can be so great that it can lead a person to deny its existence inside of oneself—which then almost inevitably leads to unconsciously projecting one's own darkness and undesirable qualities into another person or persons. My poems "What's Inside," and "The Antichrist," address this projection process.

If one decides to face and become familiar with the darkness in oneself, one then begins to "take back one's projections"—to humbly, honestly, and soberly acknowledge the darkness in oneself, and to take responsibility for expressing these dark desires in constructive ways. Doing this constructive work is indeed "work"; and it usually involves mourning the childhood traumas and emotional wounds which give rise to destructive impulses in the first place—towards oneself or towards other people.

The more a person does this constructive work, the more he or she becomes truly whole—healed from the dis-ease that results from denying, rejecting, or projecting a part of oneself. The poems "Hawkman" and "Hamlet and Me" capture something of this healing work.

This healing and wholeness usually come about as a result of being accepted and loved by another person or persons for the entirety of one's self—one's lightness and well as one's darkness. Being accepted for all of oneself, then, in turn, helps a person to feel grateful and full of love and compassion for others who are struggling on their life journey; helps one to be understanding and compassionate towards these other persons as they struggle to face and work through their own darkness on the way to wholeness or salvation. By "salvation" I mean being saved or freed from the grip of those egotistical needs and desires which can lead a person to think of themselves as "God," and then treat others condescendingly or manipulatively in order to meet their own needs, usually at others' expense. On the other hand, Jesus' relationship with his "Father" [Transcendent/God] and his way of living and relating to people are exemplary models of surrendering one's ego to Divine presence and will.

As the Psalmist asserts, much knowledge is revealed in darkness, which can be uttered in speech during the day. What a powerful poetic verse in its own right!

But my final choice for a title is "Poetry Zooms In"—which, on the face of it, makes clear that this is a book of poems; but then at a deeper level, expresses what a poem does. This title captures the ability of a poem to sharply focus on a subject or an observation and see deeply beneath the surface, to the heart of a matter. A poem helps the writer—and the reader or hearer—to slow down, focus, reflect, and meditate upon the subject being written about, while also be open to the entire range of feelings that are evoked. The subtitle, "On the Sacred in Persons and World," captures what my poems zoom in on.

A poem is an invitation to attend to the beauty, intricacy, depth, richness, or horror of whatever the poem is focusing on. A person can hopefully feel enlightened; emotionally moved; and enriched through reading or hearing the poem.

The "Transcendent" is most commonly thought of as outside or above oneself; but it is equally accurate to think of it as also deep within oneself—as, in fact, the Source of one's birth and everyday existence. Rilke puts it beautifully when he gives this advice to a young poet: "Go within and scale the depths of your being, from which your very life springs forth."[3]

"Zooming in" suggests going deep, which brings me back to the notions of the Sacred and the Mundane. In this regard, I love and

---

3. Rilke, *Letters*, 9.

agree with these words of the Historian of Religions, Mircea Eliade in his book *The Sacred and the Profane: The Nature of Religion*[4]:

> The religious . . . [person] always believes that there is an absolute reality, the sacred, which transcends this world but manifests itself in this world, thereby sanctifying it and making it real.

Eliade doesn't explicitly mention "darkness," but he sets the stage for thinking about it when he writes that the

> Modern nonreligious . . . [person] assumes a new existential situation; regards [him-or herself] solely as the subject and agent of history, and . . . refuses all appeal to transcendence . . . The sacred is the prime obstacle to [his- or her] freedom . . . [He or she] will not [in his or her own mind] be truly free until [he or she] has killed the last god.

The "nonreligious" person, to use Eliade's term, desacralizes the world, and sets up his or her ego as ultimate, which can lead to all kinds of egotism and "darkness"—such as arrogance, greed, war, anxiety, paranoia, tyranny, and even murder in order to preserve one's own narcissism and vaunted centrality.

One of my poems which addresses this "darkness" most directly is "Babies Still Sacrificed"; but "Covid Confronts Me" is also in this vein.

I believe that there is in everyone a temptation to live in the way that Eliade describes "the nonreligious" person as living; and for that reason there is the need to face the dark truth about ourselves, and then work to acknowledge and accept that truth (of wanting to regard ourselves as the sole subject and agent of history) and make ongoing efforts to "not be conformed to this world, but be transformed by the renewing of [our] minds, so that [we] may discern what is the will of God—what is good and acceptable and perfect."[5] There are also, of course, in addition to Eliade's religious and nonreligious persons, those persons who call

---

4. Eliade *The Sacred*, 202.
5. *The Holy Bible NRSV*, Romans 12:2.

themselves "religious" and claim or even believe that they have the true and inside knowledge of the will of God. But the way that they disrespect and even harm people who believe differently than them, reveals that they are actually in the same category as the "nonreligious" people, setting up their own ego or their group's ego as ultimate.

But lest you be deterred or put off by my focus on what the night reveals, let me humbly reassure you that most of my poems are suffused with deep delight, contemplative wonder, and transformative joy—each in their own now autonomous way. They're free of me. Now over to you!

In summary, I write poems as a way to see deeply into persons and the world, to see both the darkness and the light; to be mindful of the Sacred in the world even if It is being opposed or ignored, which is heartbreaking. On the other hand, it is heart-lifting and awesome to see the radiance and transformative power of the Sacred as it is manifested in nature; in human growth and development; in the healing process; in personal growth (in myself and my clients); and even in death. The poems are arranged under these headings. I hope that you savor them, see something of what I see or even more, and are fascinated by the presence of the Sacred even in something like the way that a House Wren builds its nest.

Acknowledgements

I'M GRATEFUL TO MAIREAD Stack, my partner, to whom this book is dedicated; to all those whose Endorsements grace the back cover of this book; and to all my friends, colleagues, and family members—all of whom appreciate my poems and encourage me to write.

I'm grateful again to the Editors at Wipf and Stock for accepting my Proposal and publishing this book: Matt Wimer, George Callihan, Joe Delahanty; this is the fourth book of mine which they've published, which I have found very encouraging.

Most of all, I'm grateful to the Holy Spirit, my creative Muse, which just keeps inspiring me to write!

Nature and Outdoors

Poetry Zooms In

A poem can capture a moment,
Zoom in on an instant in time
Otherwise lost in the ongoing rush
Of a life not experienced in rhyme.

In Autumn, let's say,
A fast-falling leaf
Abruptly suspended midair,
Cuts left, darts right,
Back flips, just hangs;
Then swing-dancing drunkenly down
At last comes to rest on the ground;

Poetry zooms in thus from forest tree to leaf,
Beholds with awed eyes one season of life
With childhood wonder, then sober awareness
That people fall too from the metaphor tree.

The course of a leaftime in poem or in story
Reminds one of the human seasonal journey:
From bud to pastel in the first blush of Spring
To fully formed leaves in Summer heat and storm;
Maturity in autumn brings brilliance of hue,
Then dropping into winter there's dying to do.

At minimum the body decays like a leaf
Whether burned into ash or interred into dust.
But what of the spirit: does it simply evanesce
Or return to its source the Creator to bless?

Thus a lot more is captured than an instant in time.
The instant thus captured gives motion to mind;
In simple observation there's so much to find
That only a human can write out in rhyme.

Wren Miracle

If you want
   to see a miracle,

watch a House Wren
   insert a stick—
at least the length
   of itself or longer—
into the nine-eighths inch
   diameter entrance hole
in its little house.

The miracle
   is the way
it angles its head and neck
   just so . . . just so . . .
to insert
   the front end of the stick
lengthwise,
   into the hole,
while gingerly entering
   the hole itself
alongside the stick,
   thus bringing
the rear end
   of stick and self
into the hole.

Two other aspects
    of the miracle
which amaze me
    are the wren's
confidence and
    seeming self-assurance
that it can do all this;
    and its perseverance.

It's rate of success
    is astounding!
I have seen it fail:
    by trying to insert
a forked stick
    into the hole,
or perhaps when hurrying
    or inexperienced,
it presents a stick
    crosswise across
the hole, which of course
    doesn't work.
But the wren
    will keep trying—
doesn't give up easily.

But even with a
    few failures,
it will fill that house
    with sticks,
make a nest
    of soft material
in the rear of
    the house,
lay its eggs there,
    and proceed

during the course
    of a summer
to raise two broods,
    or clutches,
of offspring—
    who in four weeks,
peek out, fledge,
    then fly away
to find their own territory.

The parents usually
    raise another clutch,
after which they are
    seen or heard no more,
having flown south
    in the autumn
to return next year
    to the very same hole!
to start all over again—
    an underrated
ordinary miracle.

The Wren's Nest

I cleaned out the wren house
At the end of the season;
Threw out the used nest,
With all of its leavings.

A couple months later,
In pre-snow December,
I happened upon the nest
Where it lay in the meadow.

For some reason, this time
Its design caught my eye:
At one end of woven sticks
The nest was softly lined.

I was filled with amaze
At this little bird's mind:
Instinctually tender?
Or love of a bird kind?

But either way really,
Intentional or not,
The layout of that nest
Suggests a tender heart.

Perhaps a little comfort
From this can be drawn:
In the midst of life's violence,
There beats a heart warm.

"Oh, ye of little faith,"[1]
We read that Jesus said;
Don't forget that the Father
Counts the hairs on your head.[2]

However, it is necessary
That the nest be in the back,
Because it's a part of creation
That death's roaming about.

One could say there's no meaning
No teleological bent:
That one lives or one dies,
The result of random events.

But I'm going with what I saw
In the design of that nest:
There's a preference for life,
Leaning towards tenderness;

That even if a snake should
Sneak in and eat an egg,
The snake too wants to live,
And the un-wren is life-food;

That everything serves Life
'cept intentional violence,
Which we're invited to stop
With vulnerable tenderness.

"Be ye wise as a serpent,
Harmless as a dove."[3]
Know what constitutes life,
But make choices from love.

1. *The Holy Bible (NRSV)*, Matthew 14:31.

2. Matthew 10:30.

3 Matthew 10:16.

Spider Web Hammock

With the dew of the misty Spring morn,
The spider-web-hammock, grass-borne,
Is lit white by the just-dawning sun.

Prey of the spider gains reprieve:
Now whitened, the trap can be seen.
Soon enough, the spider will feed.

Mid-morning the dew will be gone;
Such moments don't last very long.
Creation shines, is still, and moves on.

Ant Swarm

Fifteen of us birdwatchers
Walk quietly single-file
Down a leaf-covered trail
Along the side of a mountain
Which drops off steeply
To our right on a coffee
Plantation in Chiapas, Mexico,
In crisp late-March weather.

We're always on alert
For the voice of our leaders
—one in front and one at the rear—
To point out a native bird
For us hopefully to see
Or at least at a minimum, to hear.

As we approach a curve ahead
Which bends to our left,
The front leader suddenly yells,
"Jump to the left! Up off
The path, and be very quiet!"
As he himself does what he says.

An intense whisper
Travels from him back
Up the line, "Ant swarm!"

Hearts beating rapidly,
We all do as he says—
Looking puzzled—and wait.
We're wondering
What an ant swarm is.
But immediately
We look with awe and watch
What most of us could never
Have imagined seeing!

There's an intense rustling
Of leaves on the path
Where we had been.
The rustling approaches us,
The leaves start to move;
But they're being lifted up
From beneath, not above
Like when the wind blows.

There's a sharply defined
Front line of this movement
Approaching us,
Preceded by frantic insects
Leaping fast as they can
Off the path, only to be
Snapped up and devoured
By awaiting birds who are
Excitedly familiar with—
And clearly grateful for—
These ant swarms.

This swarm with all
Its accompanying frenzy
Passes up the path
Directly in front of us,
Just inches away,
And then it's past.

We're breathless, incredulous,
Recovering from witnessing
A primal wonder of nature:

This army of ants
Marching en masse,
Mostly invisibly
Under the leaves,
Devouring whatever
Insects aren't quick enough
To leap out of the way;
And the very birds
We've come to see
Get the rest.

Roosting In The Evergreen Trees

In my modest second home,
The only home I've owned,
I'd spend most every weekend
With my son.

My wife remained at home:
Being a clergywoman, she
Worked Sundays, was every day
On the run.

I loved my little son
From time of his adoption.
Who took most care of him?
I'm the one.

I loved taking care of him.
He hated my leaving home.
He'd say when on the phone,
"Daddy come home."

I worked five days a week:
Afternoons, four evenings, then
Friday eves he and I would leave
For country home.

I loved that mountain home;
Its small wood-burning stove
Aglow in winter kept us
Cozy and warm.

My wife and I estranged
By jobs and scheduling,
We also grew apart
Emotionally.

My wife and I surely tried
To address our deep divide;
Nothing worked and it's hard
To move on.

Colleagues whom I worked with
Were the educated class;
The people in her parish,
Working class.

We spent some family times
On occasional weekends
With a couple—our friends—
And their two sons.

In the midst of all this,
I'm sure you have guessed,
I was missing a co-parent
Companion.

Sometimes when in the country,
Though my son and I were busy,
I'd nonetheless feel achingly
So alone.

I remember this one day,
He was probably four or three,
I just couldn't stand to be
There alone.

We drove two miles away—
It was nearing end of day—
To a little group of stores
'Round a pond.

We went there fairly often;
Being there was comforting;
We'd walk, or sit on benches
Near the pond.

Just back of one bench there,
Adjacent to a store,
Some stately evergreens
Stood nearby.

As daylight now was fading,
I heard a bit of rustling
In those evergreen trees
Just behind us.

I turned around to look,
And felt profound comfort
To see chickens roosting
In those trees.

I showed them to my son,
Who was fascinated,
Hadn't grown up on a farm
As I had.

What I still find so amazing
Is how those chickens roosting
Prepared me for the darkness
Of the night.

Having grown up on a farm,
Witnessing animal rhythms,
I'd learned that all creatures
Just go on.

Those chickens had a place
Where at night they rested safe.
It brought to mind God's grace
To depend on.

With a much calmer heart
As it was getting dark,
My son and I could start
To head home.

Yes, there's loneliness and death,
But one also needs to rest,
Put the restless self to bed
In God's care.

There's day and there's night,
There's dark and there's light.
I'm a better companion
To myself.

Rustling in January

I hear some rustling as I'm walking along,
which gets my attention: I look around:
I see leaves on an oak tree—dry, curled, and brown.
It's January, and they're still hanging on!

This seems an unseasonal state of affairs,
which leads me to wonder what's going on here.
Why are those leaves still hanging on so late?
I decided some research to undertake.

Most deciduous trees drop their leaves in the Fall,
'cause leaves on the tree stop making chlorophyll.
The branches then develop abscission cells,
which cut off the dead leaves and leave the stems sealed.

This abscission zone—called a separation zone—
appears on the end of the leaf-supporting stem.
The top layer of this zone has cells with weak walls,
and the bottom layer's cells expand in the Fall.

Expansion breaks apart those cells with weak walls,
shattering to pieces what used to be whole cells;
there's nothing there left for the leaf to cling to,
so falling to the ground is all it can do.

Sometimes variations in weather conditions,
mean oaks don't develop good zones of abscission.
When this doesn't happen it's called "marescence";
then wind or heavy snow finish the business.

My casual walk on this winter's day,
my enchantment with rustling tree leaves,
led me to attend and focus more deeply
on one of Nature's intricate mysteries.

Ritual of Spring

Every Spring on a sunny day
which would be warm enough
to hang out wet clothes
on the clothesline to dry,
she'd be right out there
with a wet rag wiping
the clothesline wires clean.

Back and forth she'd walk
four times down each line—
arm and hand above her head,
wiping each of those four wires.

As a boy, watching her,
I'd think "needless work";
but one day I threw something
wet and white over the line,
and saw the black streak
left by the dirty unwiped wire:
at which point I understood.

Her cleaning was a sort of work,
but now I knew it wasn't needless.
However, what puzzled me next
was almost a spring in her step.
How could work be almost fun?
Later I realized it was the Sun
and the hope that Spring brings.

This was my Mom outside again
after being cooped up indoors
for the late Fall and Winter seasons,
now out in the sunny light
and warmth of Spring!

What looked like work
was also a guise
for getting outside
to celebrate Spring!

Corn Field Mystery

While driving along an Iowa country road
between fields, like seas, of deep green corn—
the corn being knee-high on the fourth of July,
its leaves rippling like waves in the summer breeze—

I noticed an empty spot right in the middle
of the field—a perfectly defined rectangle
approximately fifteen by fifty feet—
quite visible on the gentle slope facing me.

What in the world is that, I wondered.
I'd never seen anything like it before,
and I wondered what it could mean.
Was it perhaps an act of vandalism?

Or was it some kind of planned experiment
by the farmer, or in cooperation with him?
If I had driven by later in the season,
the taller corn might have made it invisible.

I was on an early summer visit
to my parents, so when I arrived at their house,
I asked my Dad—who was a retired farmer—
about that strange empty spot in that cornfield.

He chuckled knowingly, the way he often did,
and said, Oh, the corn planter may have stopped working
a bit, and he didn't know it—just kept going;
he'd never know it happened till the corn came up.

And you know, Son, there's no such thing as perfection.
I laughed and laughed, first of all at myself,
for taking the whole thing so seriously,
then at the farmer, the machine, life itself,

for the absurdity of thinking that
there's not imperfection in everything!
To paraphrase Robert Burns' poem "To a Mouse":
"The best laid plans of mice and men can still go wrong."

Digging Deep

I'm digging deep down,
I'm digging deep down,
is the rhythmic sound
of the well-drilling
machine.

It thumps and pounds,
thumps and pounds
with a crunching sound
as it goes up and down,
rhythmically.

The deafening sound
goes round and round
as the rocker arm
goes up and down,
endlessly.

The slag gets wet
and wetter yet
when water is hit and
comes gushing out—
finally.

The well's been dug;
it's finally done.
Water deep down
can now be drunk,
for life.

Human Growth and Development

Baby's TV

Not baby's own television set,
But six-month-old baby
Being held by mother,
Looking out the window
Fascinated
At the motion of life
Outside—
Gurgling and pointing,
Swimming the air
With its arms and legs,
But mostly just agape
With wonder at the world.

Brokering Death

A little boy sits building structures with blocks
As carefully tongue-out as he can;
Then with great energy he knocks them all down,
Making noises that sound like it's fun.

What a marvel these outward creations
That emerge from some vision within;
Then this other expression of aggression
Flattens all so he can start over again.

At age three already he's brokering death,
Unaware this'll go on all his life:
Creatively partnering proactively with death
Till he yields spirit to Spirit at last breath.

But what about someone whom life knocks around
Such that it's an effort to rebuild again?
Hopefully such a one will reach out for help,
Be rebuilt by Spirit between and within.

Little Girl at Crosswalk

While crossing a two-way street,
I looked at the little girl's eyes.
I was hurrying with a cup of tea,
Was caught by her eyes catching mine.

My heart skipped a beat and was warmed,
Those eyes showed the essence of her.
She was probably four years old,
Trying to human-eyes the world.

Waiting to cross the street she
Was holding her daddy's hand.
I'm not sure why she looked at me,
Perhaps trying to understand

How does this city world work,
How do people cross the street.
Here's daddy, but this other man
Is crossing; why should we wait?

I was crossing against the red light,
Her daddy waiting for the "Walk" sign.
She was brightly taking this in;
This was stretching her little child mind.

I saw some fear in her eyes,
Perhaps too some concern for me;
But also some surprise,
And pleasure at being seen.

We connected through our eyes,
Swapped places for a second;
I became a little child,
Safely holding daddy's hand;

She ventured into my shoes,
Imagined crossing on her own,
A little outside the rules,
Risking going it alone.

There's a time for being a child,
For holding a parent's hand.
I was reminded of just how wild
This city is even for a man.

Traffic Cop Snapshot

An enormously obese traffic cop
in a bright-yellow slicker
stands with her arms upraised
facing the flat-fronted cab
of a huge cement truck
with an all-glass double-wide
windshield, behind which
sits up high a smiling driver.

The cop seems to be enjoying her power,
behaving as if she's almost as
big as that massive truck,
as powerful as Moses of old,
whose Israelite armed forces
prevailed over their enemies
as long as his arms were raised—
which they were all day until sundown![1]

The traffic light has long since
changed to green, but she still stands
as if holding back the forces
of the universe as long as
she possibly can; then she
drops her arms and turns aside,
acknowledging in her own time
that the light has turned green,
and the world moves on again.

1. *The Holy Bible (NRSV)*, Exodus 17:8–13.

Hawkman[1]

In a quaint luncheonette in McGregor, Iowa,
with a high school classmate called Hawkman—
whom I actually hadn't known back then
because I'd rarely gotten to know underclassmen—

I began to feel some deep emotions stirring
as he and I were reminiscing now fifty years later
about classmates, teachers and the Principal whom
we independently, but similarly, remembered.

In high school, I was essentially a nerd,
constantly studying and afraid to break the rules.
He was reminding me that he was in a foursome
who were troublemakers, hellraisers—pick your word.

Though I didn't know personally the members of this group,
I knew in a peripheral sort of way about their antics—
how they'd harass unqualified, insecure, uptight teachers:
for example, rolling a softball to the front of the classroom

and looking innocent while everyone stifled laughter,
the teacher taking the bait by demanding to know who did it.
He hadn't learned that ignoring misbehavior extinguishes it,
or that laughing along builds a bond, and gives everyone a break.

Hawkman, my partner and I laughed about all this;
but then I noticed that he was becoming uncomfortable
as he reminded me that they called the Principal "Flipper,"
because his left hand hung down from his right-angled arm

1. I have received permission from "Hawkman" to publish this poem.

in such a way that it indeed flopped around like a seal's flipper,
due to his having had polio many years earlier.
We three couldn't restrain our laughter as he told this,
while being aware of how cruel and not funny it was.

At that point the tone changed:
Hawkman put his sandwich down
and began to tell us
in a different voice—
with a timbre of emotion—
what happened, what he did,
thirty or so years after
his High School graduation.

Hawkman had moved away and endured the unspeakable
losses of his adult son and three-year-old grandson—
victims of a head-on drunk-driver car crash out West
which he'd told us earlier at lunch in the same somber voice.

More about that later. Meanwhile, Hawkman had heard
that Paul the high school Principal—long since retired,
was in the hospital and would most likely not leave alive.
Whereupon Hawkman, vulnerable himself, went to visit him.

Paul was indeed not well,
clearly not long for this world.
But he greeted Hawkman warmly,
even though surprised to see him.

Hawk told him he'd heard of his condition,
And that he'd come with unfinished business—
which was to apologize for teenage meanness
which he now sincerely regretted.

Paul was gracious, grateful, forgiving,
"Hey, man, thanks so much for coming.
You were young, I was too strict.
I hope you will forgive me too."

With full hearts, they said goodbye.
It was a short visit; Paul was dying.
Now the three of us in the luncheonette—
as Hawkman told this story, were crying.

But that wasn't all. At Paul's funeral,
his wife approached Hawk to tell him
that Paul had told her of Hawk's visit
and had said that it meant the world to him.

Well of course all three of us were
watering with our tears what remained
of our luncheon food—less important
now that we'd been fully filled by Spirit.

The three of us were now bonded at a deep level,
and as we slowly finished our meal,
Hawk talked about how he and his son
had written, sung, and recorded songs together.

He himself has continued singing, song-writing;
and we heard him perform with a small band.
It's clear that this creativity is helping him
to transform his traumatic loss into new life.

To pay his bills, he works for environmental,
conservation, and bird-monitoring groups
along the Mississippi River in "The Driftless" area—
a region with dramatic terrain untouched by glaciers.

He played for a us a song he wrote called "Driftless,"
and while we were listening, he expressed delight
that his Muse had given him these lyrics,
which he couldn't imagine he or anyone would write:

"Magnetic force in the Paleozoic plateau
tugs at my spirit, resonates in my soul;
another ridge to climb, another valley to explore,
still I wanna find more . . . Driftless . . ."[2]

There is a roving, roaming quality to Hawkman:
he alights lightly, lives unconventionally,
but is fully present and disciplined in his research
of the Cerulean Warbler and the Red-shouldered Hawk.

Next day, guiding us to the Cerulean's habitat,
he talked of his years-long efforts to rescue
his estranged brother from alcoholism—
until Hawk realized the futility of rescuing.

He learned, though concerned, to stop enabling;
then watched as events beyond his control
intervened in his brother's life such that
he is now in recovery and a brother again.

The time with Hawkman that weekend
helped me see and feel again
the healing presence of Holy Spirit
in brokenness as well as creativity.

I never knew Hawkman in High School,
but now I'll never forget him.
He's responded to the tragedies of life
with emotional and spiritual maturity.

My favorite song of his goes like this:
"Way down yonder in the mystery,
Following the light of my destiny
Leaves my soul feeling oh so free."[3]

---

2. Stravers, Jon. "Driftless." *Hawkman Solo.*
3. Stravers. "Rainbow Warrior." *Hawkman Solo.*

Menopause

Menopause:
A "failure
Of the system?"
Actually, no.
More so:
A potential
Time of
Transformation.

Procreation
No more.
Reproduction's
Over. That's that.
But Creativity:
Is that over?
Of that kind, yes.
But wait . . .

Reducing
Woman's worth
To physiology,
Body biology,
Leaves so much out.
Is a woman's value
Merely "Usefulness?"
Restricted to that?

In patriarchy, sadly,
Too easily, yes.
But thankfully,
There's more,
Much more!
The menopausal
woman lives on,
And menopause
Becomes a metaphor.

There's more to life
Than procreation.
Some systems die,
But life goes on.
Death is not the end,
But a creative door
To transformation
To a Higher Order.

When menopause happens,
People have a choice:
To focus on death,
The end of woman's worth;
Or to open our eyes,
To hear the voice
Of Life beyond life,
The Life of Source.

Open eyes can see
That preparation
And procreation
Involve both
Male and Female:
Female openness,
Receptivity; and
Male penetration,
donation:

Partnering in the
Generation of life,
Then in maternal
Protection and maintenance
Of intrauterine conditions
Conducive
To embryonic growth
Until fetal birth.

All this is literally true,
But also a metaphor:
For loving warmth,
Respectful openness
And receptivity by
Male and Female of
The Spirit's penetrating
Animation of life on earth.

Partnering
As metaphor:
Male and Female
Cooperating together
With Spirit Source
To create conditions
Conducive to safety
For all kinds of life.

"Metaphor" helps
Explain "reborn":
Born by Spirit
To greater awareness
That there's more to life
Than what we see
Or can control,
Including death.

Painful as it is,
Can we embrace
Change and death
As not the end?
Death of one system
In a larger context
Makes it possible to
Value life AND death.

It truly is very scary
To not be in control.
We forget to remember
To partner with Source,
To surrender our pride,
In humble posture
Kneel. Then stand tall!
Empowered spiritually

To embrace
Even death
As necessary
Tilling of soil,
Breaking open
The surface
To let life
In and out.

The prophet Micah
Tells what is good:
"Do justice [treat
Everyone as equal],
Love mercy [forgive
Male and female pride],
And walk humbly
With our God."[1]

1. *The Holy Bible (NRSV)*, Micah 6:8.

Illness and Healing

Dizzy

I've been feeling dizzy lately
as I arise from lying down.
Aging and medicine suggest
blood pressure up or down;
occluded coronary arteries;
restricted flow of spinal fluid.

My rising sign being Virgo,
I leapt to those possibilities.
But my homeopathic doctor—
reading and discussing my chart—
spoke from within that system
in an almost throwaway line:

"Lots of energies circling around
up there." The line landed within
me, and along with other things
happening in my life, I'm thinking
that this surge of creative energy,
since I began writing poetry—

arising from the generative
unconscious within or through me—
may be making me dizzy
as I've accepted this new identity
as a writer of narrative poetry
in addition to doing psychotherapy.

The affirmation of publication
has been at times intoxicating—
heady—especially as I've undertaken
to give expression to mystery,
which calls upon the artist's craft
in service to what is beyond me.

Recovery Room Nurse

I had agreed to the Green Light
Laser treatment of my prostate—
to remove its impingement
upon my urethra, which made it
difficult to urinate and made my
bladder so full of urine that it
was backing up into my kidneys.

The kidney pain drove me
to an Emergency Room
at one o'clock in the morning.
They did a c-t scan,
diagnosed the problem,
and inserted a catheter,
complete with a leg bag—
after draining my bladder
of an amazing amount of urine!

In the next few days,
I found an Asperger-y Urologist
who specialized in Robotics
(and behaved somewhat
like a robot himself,
which in the end was
to my advantage).

He prescribed the laser treatment;
sent me to a Primary Care Physician;
did an exploratory cystoscopy;
then scheduled the surgery.
He'd been highly recommended,
and the cystoscopy was painless,
so I entrusted myself to his
and the Anaesthesiologist's care
for the Green Light treatment.

Admission to the hospital
went smoothly, with its waits
and silly chilly open-back gowns,
data-gathering, and the Intern's
telling me what would happen.

An Orderly wheeled me
down the hall, bumping
around corners, into the
brightly-lit operating room.
Nurses all around the
doctor's face, inserted
an intravenous port
into my left hand,
asked if I was ready, and
said I'd soon go to sleep.

I must have.

Next thing I knew,
I faintly heard as in a dream
the softest, sweetest voice
calling my name.
I answered like a little boy,
"Yes?" Dreamily coming awake,
mumbling, "Oh, is it all over?"

"Yes, it is, and you're fine,"
she said—this sixty-something
short, white-haired woman,
quiet, demure, tending to
another patient next to me
while inviting me to wake.
"You're in Recovery," she said,
"just relax for a while.
Your partner will be here soon."

Sure enough, my partner
soon came in, and I was
infinitely relieved to see her.
She reported that the doctor
had come bounding to her
like a little kid excitedly
telling her that everything
went well, better than expected.

I knew my partner of course
and I love her desperately;
but I hadn't even known this
Recovery Room nurse—
who was somehow an angel—
who it seemed to me
had gently called me
back from the dead.

She was the human link—
the bridge—between oblivion
and the world of the living;
the perfect person in that room,
the perfect quiet voice
inviting me back to consciousness.

As I write this, I realize that
her face and gentle demeanor
reminded me of my mother,
and maybe at some deep level
echoed me seeing my mother's face
and hearing her voice after birth—
after coming alive through her.

The mystery of it all!
Birth, life, pain, healing.
Doctors, nurses, loved ones,
the healing-Holy Spirit—
all of whom, in concert,
make wholeness happen.

Her Smile

It's a trite thing to say, yes, I know,
but it's true I believe nonetheless,
that more can be said with a smile
than words could ever express.

Coming home when I walk through the door,
she'll often be waiting just inside,
and before I can even say hello,
she'll already be giving me that smile.

Most often there follows then a kiss,
which touches me literally for sure;
but to be honest her smile moves me more,
and of all things is what I'd most miss.

I'm pondering and wondering why:
I'm thinking that the reason runs deep:
the infant lives to see its mother smile:
its body wriggles and gurgles in speech!

Seems we're wired to be seen and be touched;
without smiles babies fail to thrive.
Studies show that if infants aren't touched
they actually become listless and die.

As adults too we still have that need.
My partner's smile lights up my life.
There's a spiritual layer too I believe:
In the smile of another I see God.

Ringing in My Ears

One day I noticed a ringing in my ears,
semi-consciously assumed it would disappear.
When it didn't, I felt increasingly fear—that
it was a symptom of something more serious.

I tried to remember when it had started,
even wondered if it had been there all along—
if what had been background noise before
was now for some reason clearly foreground.

For several days it was always on my mind,
Though I forgot it when I was occupied:
my awareness of it then would subside
until I would pause or was in bed at night.

I was relieved that my hearing remained acute,
but felt increasingly anxious when it didn't heal.
Previous maladies were things one could treat,
but Tinnitus left me feeling very vulnerable.

That was the name of what I self-diagnosed
after scouring websites such as WebMD
and Mayo Clinic—both of which disclosed
that it could be permanent—no remedy.

I didn't want to accept that as the final word;
besides, I think illnesses have deeper meaning.
But I did feel betrayed by my body not healing
and disturbed by an awareness of mortality.

I began to face the possibility
that this was something
over which I had no control.
Finally, at that point, I listened

to an inner voice saying, "You need help."
Whenever that happens, I do reach out;
I call my homeopathic doctor,
which is always the right decision.

When I explained to him what
was happening, he agreed that
yes, it sound like Tinnitus.
I of course jumped too quickly

to asking if there's a remedy . . . .
He asked what's been going on
for me spiritually. Knowing him
as I do, I wasn't surprised.

I teared up, choked, could not speak.
Deep inside I knew Spirit was the issue.
When I could talk, I spoke
of how a few days previously

I had been lying in bed listening
to my favorite hymns,
and found myself overwhelmed
with this love for my clients.

I felt this powerful connection
to Divine Spirit and my clients,
that I was a bridge as a Therapist
between them and healing Spirit.

Suffused, I felt then, with joy and peace,
profoundly grateful to be doing therapy,
rested, refreshed, and re-energized
in a timeless way full of mystery.

Well somehow, he said,
that's what this is about.
Notice, when I asked you
just what you talked about.

The remedy you seek is to surrender
to what the Spirit is doing through you:
the Tinnitus may or may not go away,
but listening to God is what you need to do.

My ears are still ringing;
I'm just letting it be. Mostly don't notice.
I still hear clearly; and I continue
to love and be amazed at what I do—

or, more accurately, I'm amazed
at what the Spirit does through me,
when I'm in tune with Its presence
between the client and me.

I've had the fantasy that this ear-ringing
is some extrasensory communication
from the Spirit to keep me mindful
to stay tuned in to Its frequency.

The Dark Depths

Why Didn't I Smile?

Why didn't I smile?
Oh why didn't I smile?
It would've been so easy,
As the woman walked by.

I was waiting for the train
On an autumn morning,
Noticing an elderly woman
Approaching on the platform.

She passed three or four others
As she was walking along;
Had a poised calm presence,
But her eyes held a longing.

I guess I was scared
She'd want something of me.
I glanced at her but then
Looked away instantly.

Just before I looked away,
Our eyes made contact,
She started to smile,
But I couldn't turn back.

But certainly I could have.
I'm still feeling bad.
Such an easy thing to do;
I was such a hard-ass.

Why didn't I just smile?
I can still see her face:
How her countenance fell
When I looked away.

Why didn't I just smile?
The question haunts me.
She walked on undaunted,
But she's still here with me.

Standing in the suburbs,
I was in my City head.
I couldn't switch back
Before it happened.

Babies Still Sacrificed

I was not prepared for the devastating impact
of watching on film[1] King Herod's minions
with their heavy clubs and drawn swords
chasing women who were clutching their babies
running and stumbling every which way
trying desperately to prevent impending horror,

screams their only defense as soldiers forcibly
ripped the babies from their clasping arms
and brutally hacked, stabbed, or beat them to death—
not just a few but dozens maybe hundreds,
leaving the babies' mothers prostrate
and desolately sobbing on the ground.

I'd read and heard this story from the Bible
at least once a year for over sixty years
of Christmases, but seeing it visually
and not just imaginatively in my mind
left me breathless with visceral shock,
desperately with the mothers wanting it to stop.

While watching, I immediately thought with horror
of what's been happening right now
in two-thousand-nineteen on the southern border
by agents of the Immigration and Customs
Enforcement Agency of the United States:

1. *The Gospel According to Saint Matthew*, directed by Pier Paolo Pasolini, 1965.

maybe not killing the infants but violently
ripping them from their parents' clasping arms,

now as then victimizing babies, using babies
as pawns to preserve the fragile and paranoid
ego of a leader trying to preserve his power—
a leader with his coterie of supporters who
keep him in power for their own self-interest;

a leader totally divorced of course from his own
inner child—denying its vulnerability
and dependency while trying to preserve
its grandiose infantile omnipotence,
which, unchecked, in the body of an adult,
can lead to awesome devastation.

I feel the same visceral revulsion
as I write this as when I saw the film—
a shock and recoil I can barely contain,
along with outrage and helplessness
as the machine of human obscene
cruelty rumbles and crunches on,

the leaders and perpetrators
actually continuing to authorize
and participate in the ongoing momentum
of dismembering body parts and families
who are already deprived, powerless,
and victimized, simply trying to survive.

Why, why, why?

The relentless cruelty has a life of its own,
its authors at a heartless, soulless distance
from the babies and themselves.

Feeding Time

In a mind-numbing thrall
To a dreamy-like trance
Which threatens to shatter
If I move the least muscle,

I indulge this haunted mood
Which pulls me way back
Via tenacious old roots
To an infant-child time.

I'm lying there then;
Nobody else here,
And nobody comes
To my wailing and longing.

My body's immobile,
Dull ache in my gut;
Head heavy and lolling,
I'm utterly alone.

Will food stop the aching?
But food does not come.
Will food maybe say that I am?

Now somebody's holding me,
Somebody's hurting me.
This pain lets me know that I am!

Alone again, fed.
Relieved but afraid.
The milk-bottle nipple,
Quite roughly inserted,
I sucked in the food and the pain.
Milk was ingested with pain.

Crying and choking, trying to scream
About milk being given with pain!
Enraged while I'm held
With a bit of warm softness,
Resisting both contentment
And connection through pain.

All innocence gone:
My rage wants to kill,
To detonate body and pain.
But sucking is such pleasure
And succor is seductive;
I yield to the mix that I am.

My body's my world,
My body's now calm,
I sink into peace:
Alone with myself.
My underworld's sad,
But I feel more surely "I am."

Sighing I waken,
The trance is now broken,
My neck muscles loosen,
My lungs are now open,
I'm breathing again;
Through breath I'm enlivened.

Truth and Abuse

As soon as I say
"It's not true, it's not true!"
I'm facing the truth, but
Run back to the lie.

Denial has cracked,
But I run right back
And I try hard to act
As when living the lie.

After that I'm haunted;
I don't want to see
What happened to me.
Please let it not be.

But I know deep inside
That I don't want to hide,
That seeing sets me free,
Plus, you hearing me,

I have less need to hide
I dare live outside.
To be with my pain
Is to be whole again.

To a heart badly broken,
A trust that's betrayed:
The prophet has spoken,
"Do not be dismayed."[1]

1. *The Holy Bible (NRSV)*, Jeremiah 17:18b

What's Inside?

God confronts Adam:
Did you eat of The Tree?
It's Eve whom you gave me,
He says, she seduced me.
But wait! He avoids looking
At the rebel within him.

The Twin Towers are hit.
Let's not wonder why.
We've gotta lash out
With our military!
We hardly dare ask
About the enemy within.

God prefers my brother!
Fumes Cain about Abel.
Instead of changing his ways,
He clubs to death Abel;
He even looks within but still doesn't stop
The horror of which he's capable.

That man looks like a Muslim;
Therefore we can't trust him.
All Muslims are evil;
Jihad's their religion.
The evil's out there,
There's no evil within.

A coat of many colors!
Dad clearly prefers him.
We'll kill him, make Dad hurt
The way we're hurting.
They do it without checking
The power of envy within.

Gripped by unquestioned racism,
White cop provokes a situation
Which confirms his inner fear
Of the black man as demon;
Feels justified in killing him,
Denying the demon's within.

Perceiving the Other as Enemy
Is best considered a sign
That what we're seeing out there
Is a projection of stuff within,
Leaving us in imminent danger
Of ourselves becoming the demon.

The Antichrist Within

The Antichrist in every Christian,
can be triumphantly disowned,
projected onto others with venom
to not see the devil as one's own.

It's human to resist the Holy Spirit:
doing so helps define who we are—
gives us the distance to be a free agent
who can then choose for oneself or for God.

Mature growth in one's relationship with God
is to acknowledge what used to be called sin:
that like Adam and Eve we want to BE God,
not accept the creature choice we've been given.

Jesus himself models how hard it can be
to surrender to divine will for one's life:
in anguish sweating blood in Gethsemane
he protests what he knows must be death.

Even with company he struggles alone,
with a choice so heavy the others fall asleep;
he knows that the choice is his own,
that he'll endure the ensuing suffering.

Though Peter resorts to violence,
Jesus won't see the enemy outside;
teaches Peter that his sword is no defense:
that the harder thing is to suffer inside.

When seeing the Antichrist as only outside,
a person fears it and tries to subdue it,
or at best ties to persuade or convert it,
leaving one standing in self-righteous pride.

Christians risk becoming most unlike Jesus
when they project their own resistance outside.
Church history and some church-state alliances
reveal the shame of Christians being Antichrist.

The Christian who wants to challenge Antichrist
would do best to take back his/her projections,
for it's only by getting to know one's own demons
that there can be inner or outer transformation.

This is an arduous road for anyone,
and one usually needs a spiritual guide,
to support one's desire for transcendence
and the surrendering of egotistical pride.

Covid Confronts Me

My heart is sad and heavy, Covid.
Seeking relief, I become angry.
I wonder if you're angry, Covid;
I wonder, is your essence heavy?

I'm angry that you're bothering me;
but we humans, I know, invaded you;
we violated nature's boundaries,
opening ourselves to invasion by you.

The balance of life is sorely askew;
there's loss of meaning spiritually.
The gods we worship are power and greed,
self-exaltation; no humility.

I think I might be beginning to know,
I think I may be starting to see:
you're not the enemy I need to know,
you're helping me see the enemy in me.

You got my attention by making me sick;
I think you're the problem, certainly not me!
But the more I learn of what's going on,
I realize you're confronting me with me.

Harmless you were in your own habitat,
but bored human beings sought something new:
killed pangolins for scales, disrupted the bats:
your homes now destroyed, we became your new food.

But humans and Covid aren't meant to be
helping each other symbiotically.
Instead we're engaged in a life and death fight;
will even all these deaths help us see the light?

I'm a dealer in death, in disrespect:
I've failed to respect life's intricacy:
I need to respect life's intricate web,
to worship, be humble, sacrifice greed.

Personal Growth

Threshold Thoughts

My ninety-year-old house threshold was rotten.
Replacing it, as I had feared, became daunting.
The websites that I studied for guidance
hadn't prepared me for the necessary violence.

I had known that the cottage was well-built,
but hadn't a clue what, in this case, that meant.
The metal piece on top of the rotted wood
had to come off before I could proceed.

With ease I removed the two visible screws—
only to be puzzled when it still wasn't loose.
The door jambs and doorstops had to come off,
and by that point I resorted to cursing.

I couldn't believe what I finally observed:
four nails from outside the bottom of the doorframe
tightly and precisely inserted into the metal threshold
like screws into two nail-sized cavities at each end!

My frustration at this point barely knew bounds:
those nails were like screws: couldn't be pulled out!
I placed the claws of a crowbar on top of each nail,
banged violently with my hammer, refusing to fail.

With this kind of pounding the nails finally broke,
releasing the metal piece and giving me hope.
The rest of the process was comparatively easy:
removing the wooden part and repairing things neatly.

The three days it took me to complete this project
gave me plenty of time to ponder and reflect
about the fact that a threshold marks inside and out:
that almost every existing thing has an inside and out.

The rotting threshold needing to be replaced
prompted me to think about something so basic:
boundaries—even underfoot—taken for granted,
but without which nothing would have definition.

Are boundaries in fact the essence of creation?
The biblical story is all about definition:
each creation step, things are being separated:
a "formless void" but also a God who's creating.[1]

"In the beginning God"—the original Oneness—
"created the heavens and the earth"—already two.
Even in the act, there is God the one Being
instantly separate from what God produces.

Boundaries are immediately there by definition,
but they don't necessarily cause isolation:
a boundary defines and separates, yes,
but each of those sides is also adjoining.

The light from the darkness, God separates;
the earth from the sky; ocean from dry land;
vegetation, fruit, and the seeds of new life;
sea creatures and earth creatures, multiplying!

It's a story that's bursting abundantly with life
in ever increasing variety and intricacy,
culminating in the creation of conscious human
beings, formed from dirt, animated, breathing.

---

1. *The Holy Bible (NRSV)*, Genesis 1:1—2:3.

These humans created in the image of God—
have layers of being, animated by Spirit:
unconscious depths full of raw materials,
conscious minds able to destroy and create.

I destroyed and created my threshold;
The process engaged body, mind, and spirit.
I'm grateful that I'm created in God's image—
able to be creative, and see projects finished.

Afraid to Preach

Having decided
while in college
to study for the ministry,
I applied
and was accepted
to Princeton Seminary.

A major thing
ministers do,
of course is to preach,
but I was
literally terrified
of public speaking.

While delivering
the mandatory speech
in high school,
I had had an
almost dissociative
experience.

In the two required
Speech classes
in college,
I somehow
very stiffly
muddled through.

I knew I'd be required
to take at least two
Preaching Classes
in Seminary,
which knowledge left
a gnawing dread
in my gut.

I avoided taking those classes
as long as possible—
rationalizing that I would
opt to be an Associate Pastor
or find a Pastoral job that
didn't involve preaching.

But taking one of those
classes was inevitable,
so I chose the soft-spoken
more mild-mannered
Professor whom I felt
least intimidated by.

It never occurred to me
to talk to him or
anyone else about my fears.
But it didn't take long
for his experienced eye
to see that I was in trouble.

He had laid a solid
physiological foundation
for how to use one's diaphragm
to relax, breathe deeply,
and project one's voice
while speaking in public.

This was new and helpful
information for me;
but even so, after I'd read—
in a mortified monotone—
some poetry and scripture
he'd given us to read in class,

he pulled me aside one day
to say that there was
a Faculty Associate
whom he thought
could be helpful to me—
a retired female actress

named Virginia Damon;
that I should contact her
for a Speech lesson. I did.
We met—just the two of us—
in this immense
corner room upstairs

in ancient ugly Stuart Hall.
The thick stone walls
were like pillars between
many elongated windows
which soared upward
towards the sky-high ceiling.

Ms. Damon—standing at my level
between the desk on its dais
and the door—suggested that
I go across the enormous room,
stand looking out the window,
and just tell a story, any story.

This radically unconventional
arrangement in this staid
but spacious old room in a
revered theological seminary
shocked me out of my superego
to think maybe I could think for myself.

I felt for the first time free
of the daunting responsibility
of preaching God's Word.
She was inviting me
to tell my own story—
any story I chose!

I momentarily drew a blank,
but as I stood looking out
the window, I saw a squirrel,
and I began to tell about
how I used to hunt squirrels—
shot and killed them for sport.

Having grown up on a farm in Iowa,
my Dad had given me permission—
when I turned sixteen—
to buy my own single-shot rifle,
which in that place and time,
was not uncommon.

I loved hunting,
and became a good shot.
I'd walk a quarter-mile
alone to the back pasture—
free for a few hours,
from Dad, farm work, and chores.

It was peaceful being amongst
the ancient oak and maple trees,
waiting patiently for a squirrel
to poke its head out of a hole
in a tree, then take aim and shoot.
More often than not, I'd hit it.

But something deep inside
began to bother me: why
am I doing this? Rationalizing
that squirrels were plentiful, I
continued hunting for a few more months,
but soon accepted that I'd lost the heart for it.

I had loved the challenge
of hitting the target; but
trying to outwit a squirrel—what
kind of cheap rigged odds was that?
I didn't need nor eat the meat,
so I gave it up. I quit hunting.

I'd become increasingly clear
that what I loved most
was the peace and quiet—
being by myself in nature,
free of my brothers, the watchful
eye of my Dad, and work.

When I finished telling this story,
I felt somehow redeemed—
both because I had stopped hunting then,
but more because I'd found something
new in myself now: an inner grounding
in this personal experience

of the Spirit's patient presence—
incarnate in Virginia Damon:
congratulatory, warmly affirming,
conveying that she knew I could do it.
This was a one-time experience,
the mere beginnings of confidence,

but a pivotal step in my journey
of tuning the instrument of my body
and beginning to believe—have hope—
that I might become more adequate
to the task of public speaking
and a bit less afraid of preaching.

Pastor Learns a Lesson

Rain blown by a roaring wind
lashed the windows of my church office
as I was wrapping up a counseling session
with a frightened almost homeless woman
in her early thirties seeking a calm center
amidst the winds and storms of her life.

Anxiously gathering her pocketbook
and coat, she said, "Oh, its pouring outside;
I didn't bring an umbrella. Do you
have one?" "No, I'm sorry," I lied,
with a sick feeling in my stomach as I
killed human compassion by opting
for self-interest and some rigid rule
about me a Counselor not bailing her out,

thinking: "She needs to take care of herself."
Plus, I selfishly didn't want to get wet.
She left, but she didn't leave my mind.
I thought of her all that night
And to this day—as you hear—with regret.

When discussing the session two weeks later
with my supervisor, he listened, then asked,
"And did she come back for her next session?"
That sickish feeling in my stomach returned
as I shamefully said "No," and felt
convicted by the "right" thing I had done.

Hamlet and Me

I recently saw a powerful performance
Of Shakespeare's well-known play Hamlet:
I was wowed by the beauty, rhythm,
And enchantment of the language—
Even the delivery of those phrases that
Have become part of ordinary parlance,
Such as "To be or not to be—
That is the question" or "Something's
Wrong in the state of Denmark."

Benedict Cumberbatch played an
Excellent Hamlet in all dimensions:
Being young, emotionally convincing,
Clearly enunciating
Tongue-twisting phrases,
Anguishing over the ultimate question
Of whether in the face of familial
And political corruption and
Opportunistic maneuvering
Life is worth living.

My partner and I discussed all this
In a satisfying way afterwards.
Then sometime between the
Middle of the night and the
Next morning, I began to get it—
To really get the Play:
To feel and understand
Hamlet in my bones.

It seems so obvious now:
How would I too not be stricken
And tormented over what I could
Or would do if my father's brother
Poisoned and killed my father
And a month or two later
Was sleeping with my mother?!

Critics kick around the question
Of why Hamlet didn't act,
Take action, revenge his
Father's death by killing his uncle?

It dawned on me that that's
A dusty academic question
Debated at a distance from
The actual situation.

For one thing, young Hamlet
Would have been not only enraged
But, even more so, disoriented—
Torn loose from his moorings
By the fact of his mother's
Virtual approval if not collusion
In her husband's death,
And her too soon subsequent
Consorting with the murderer.

Is nothing sacred,
He'd have wondered,
If the marriage bed can be so
Lasciviously and licentiously
Violated? Another dimension
Of Hamlet's inner tumult
Would have been intensified
By the oedipal dynamic.

If in fantasy he had envisioned
Killing his father to have
His mother all to himself—
Especially with her agreement—
How could he righteously sit
In judgment on a man
Who'd beaten him to it?

But what woke me up
Was this: the helpless aspect
Of his helpless rage!
When those at the top
Of a kingdom, a country,
Or a family, take justice
Into their own hands,
It's enraging, but then
Whom can one appeal to?

To whom could he look for support?
His fiancé Ophelia's father—
Out of complicit self-interest—
Turned even her against him,
And he had no other extended
Family to turn to. Another
Level of helplessness was
Due to the fact that
The worst had already happened,
And to avenge death with death
Wouldn't heal the situation.

Hamlet didn't want
In the end to be violent.
Enough of that! But ancient
Eye-for-an-eye retaliation
Was urging him to vindicate.

So what can he do
In the midst of feeling
Helpless and enraged
Except to rail against
The "slings and arrows
Of outrageous fortune?"

That such things happen
In the world of humans, and
That the only seeming solution
Is to take up the sword
Of retribution, would prompt
A person who wanted to
Break out of this cycle
To ask the ultimate question:
"To be or not to be?"
Do I even want
To go on living?

After thinking through all of this,
I was aware of an unsettled
Inner fuzziness and sadness
Which I still didn't
Fully understand until the next
Morning when I revisited
The helpless rage feeling,
And made the connection
To the helpless rage I felt
As a little child when my
Father would hit me.

I found his behavior extremely
Disorienting, and since my mother
Didn't protect me nor even privately
Indicate that his treatment
Was unjust, I had no one

To appeal to. I felt helpless
While trying to manage rage—
Which I ended up turning
Against myself—in addition to
Feeling shame and humiliation,
With no way of being vindicated.

Hamlet confronted his mother—
Which I never even did—but
In the course of raging against
Her reluctance to admit her
Own abomination, Hamlet
Impulsively—in the grip of rage—
Stabs whom he thinks is his uncle
Hiding behind a curtain listening.
It turns out to be Ophelia's
Father Polonius that he killed,
Leading to the ultimate insult and
Mockery that even a somewhat
Mad retributive action is a failure.

So Hamlet too has blood on
His hands, and in the end—
After hearing of Ophelia's suicide
And witnessing his mother's also—
He in a fury enacts revenge
By killing his uncle and
Finally turning his sword
Upon himself.

Greater political order
Is restored with the arrival—
In Shakespearean fashion—
Of Fortinabras, King of Norway,
Who—along with the Viewer—
Is shocked at the carnage.

He then takes charge and
Proceeds to protect the area.

For me, rage
At outrageous violations
By humans in this world
Is a healthy emotion,
And the help for my
Helplessness has been
"Wording" it out in psychotherapy,
And in writing this poem,

Finding in psychotherapy
A compassionate presence
Created a safe context
Within which I could acknowledge
That I myself have been
In some ways just like my father,
Which enabled me to forgive
Both myself and my father.

"Forgiveness" being a humble
Acceptance of my humanity—
As well as my father's—
With all of its dark impulses
As well as its potential for
A relationship with Divinity,
Which helps us be clear about
Right relationship, enabling us
To be compassionate and neither
Vindictive nor condemnatory
Towards ourselves or others.

My uncle did not kill my father
Nor did my mother sleep with
Such a betrayer, so my rage

Hardly held a candle to
The maddening rage of Hamlet.

But my degree of dismay
At the end of the Play
And its lingering quality
Led me to de-repress
The helpless aspect
Of my rage at my father
For abusing me,
And at my mother
For not protesting,
Nor protecting me.

It was only after feeling
And accepting my rage
Without acting it out
That I could feel less helpless,
Because I realized that
Accepting my rage and not
Acting it out destructively
Were themselves actions—
Empowering choices,
Which meant that I was
No longer helpless now the
Way I had been as a child.

In restoring an honest,
Right relationship with myself
And my own humanity,
I was free of a need to
Retaliate or punish myself,
And able to go on living.

I didn't need to kill myself
Or anyone else in order to

Restore right relationships.
But there is a sacrifice involved.

The necessary sacrifice is
Letting go of one's primitive
Ego desires and satisfactions,
Which is made possible
Only by accepting one's
Own darkness and choosing
The Divine way over our own.
Shakespeare's play makes clear
How hard this is to do.

The Play is indeed a tragedy
With very little comic relief—
And that certainly not at the end.
But might Shakespeare be
Putting on display
The pointless vanity and
Tragedy of following
The unmitigated, unregulated
Human instincts of lust and power?
As well as suggesting some hope
In a restoration of justice and order
When major wrongs are righted—
Even if that happens
Through Hamlet's and his mother's
Self-sacrificial suicide.

These literal killings
Symbolize the depth
Of the dramatic journey
Of coming to terms with
The darkness of one's humanity,
And the difficulty of handling
One's powerful ego desires
In a non-destructive way.

Not being transformed
Results in tragedy.

Tragedy, tragedy indeed,
And a dark Play for that.
But Shakespeare refused too easy
Forgiveness and redemption
For such heinous
Yet still current crimes.

The Play is a reminder of
The devastating consequences
Of such selfish betrayals,
And offers both a catharsis
And an example of
Finding constructive ways
Of dealing with helpless rage—
One of which is to
Create and/or read, perform,
Or watch works of Art
Such as poems or plays.

These help us recognize
Ourselves in the characters,
Be brutally honest with ourselves,
And give us a bit of distance
To hopefully make healthy choices.

Death and Transformation

Deer Kill

Walking in the woods along a stream one day,
we came across what once had been coyotes' prey.
In a wildly twisted tangle of fallen tree branches—
over which we clambered with great difficulty—
there lay in a small clearing the strewn remains
of a white-tailed deer who had met its destiny.

Ribcage and leg bones were stripped hungrily clean—
no surprise in that, but something about the scene
was suddenly disconcerting: how safe were we?
If surrounded right now, could we get away?

I was on high alert now; knew I'd never forget
the brownish now white fur, laid out like a carpet
underneath disconnected, strangely long-looking
bones, twisted and tossed about in scary contortions.

We didn't see the skull—it was probably snatched away
after a growling coyote tussle over which one held sway,
The scene left a chill: we didn't linger or stay.
While leaving I thought, "I've seen enough death today."

Death Is Weird

It's an uncanny thing
How death comes to bring
These changes to how we live life.

When it snatches someone away,
Things are never the same,
Yet life goes on quite normally.

This colleague of mine
I'd known for thirty years
Hadn't seemed ill, then one day died.

Has the person gone away?
Yes, he's permanently gone;
We'll never again ride the subway.

Yet I don't just forget
Those long rides we took:
We'd stand in the subway and talk.

We'd come from a meeting—
We were on the same committee—
And ride the train home to our stops.

We didn't talk about the meeting,
But about our vacations, and
Compared notes about various stuff.

We had seen each other weekly
In groups or other meetings,
As colleagues on an Institute faculty.

So why do I remember him,
Riding together on that train,
When I'll never ever see him again?

It's death that's between us,
Yet death also links us;
It's the gate he's on the opposite side of.

He's exited this life's door,
No longer of this life form;
But his hologram inhabits my mind.

What's the nature of our being?
It's more than we can see.
What is this inner psychic life?

A structure for the soul,
An abode for the spirit,
Life-Source indwelling me?

The human body when animate
Is enlivened by spirit:
Breath inhabits this body for a time.

Yet it's all of a piece: body,
Breath, spirit, psyche.
Death's null has gotten me thinking.

It's definitely a mystery,
Has been throughout history.
Some lives leave, others remain.

Death threatens life's meaning,
But Life goes on teeming;
Corpses even fertilize life.

Yes, my personal death
Will be the end of "my" breath;
But was it ever mine anyway?

There's so little that's mine:
I'm dependent all the time
On Life-Source breathing in me.

Mom's Last Breath

Mom lay bedridden
and unresponsive
in hospice care
for ten days

before she died.
In all that time
she neither ate nor drank
nor made a sound.

For the final three days
she lay on her back
her mouth wide open,
her jaw slack.

My Dad (her husband),
and my two brothers
and their spouses
were taking turns

waiting and watching
inside the room with her,
or outside an open door
on the porch.

After all these days,
with no obvious change,
somehow the hospice nurse
knew the end was near.

She called everyone
into the room;
and as the last two
were approaching,

Mom suddenly gave
a loud cry,
her mouth
snapped shut,

And she was gone.
That was the end.
She breathed
no more.

A Strange Thing

Here's a strange
Unexpected thing:
I perceived my Dad
Differently after he died.

My image of him now was,
Of course, more from memory
And reconstruction
Than living interaction—

An image less amenable
To modification
Since he was no longer
Physically present.

When alive, there's a kind of
Psychic energy field
Emanating from a living
Person that predominates,

Which creates a subtle distance,
And an unconscious need to
Maintain one's own identity
In the presence of the other.

This dynamic is especially true
In the relationship between
A parent and their offspring:
There's a generational boundary

Which is always present,
No matter how old the child,
Which I was always aware of
Whenever I was with him.

Besides, it can be intimidating,
Intrusive, and objectifying
To study someone's face
When they're alive,

Unless you're intentionally
Painting or photographing
Them into an image
Frozen in time.

After my Dad died,
He became less
"Dad" somehow:
More like a peer.

The elevation,
Authority, hierarchy
Of the "Dad" position gone—
A loss and a gain.

And I noticed a shift from
Focusing on his appearance
To remembering
His way of being alive.

All this was triggered by,
For the first time, truly
Noticing the mole
Next to his nose

As he was lying dead
In his coffin.
I'd seen that mole
A million times

On the lower right
Side of his nose.
But I'd never seen it
This way before.

It grabbed me that day;
A tightness in my chest.
Now that he's gone I see it,
For the first and last time.

It made me wonder
What else I hadn't
Ever truly seen
About him.

Now, I began to remember
How he walked,
How he sat and
How he talked.

I'm remembering now
The way he would walk
Those five years prior
To dying at eighty-nine:

Shoulders slightly stooped,
Arms hanging straight
Down, not swinging
By his sides as he moved.

More and more he shuffled,
And I often feared he'd stumble
And fall face-forward on the floor,
unable to brace himself.

As a very young man
In his wedding photo,
He stands straight and tall,
Six-foot-two.

But when he'd sit down lately,
It was not graceful at all:
He'd back up to his recliner,
Then just drop.

His elderly legs
Were no longer limber,
Couldn't bend and hold him
As he sat down.

When sitting down to table,
He could be more graceful;
His arms would help ease him
Down onto a chair.

More often he'd talk as if
He were emerging from
A considered reverie,
Offer his conclusion,

Or maybe ask a question;
Seemingly disengaged
But then at times engaging,
Usually opinionated,

But more frequently
In those later years
A bit more tentative,
Less need to prove

His certainty,
More willing to let
Some doubt and
Listening emerge.

This was poignant to see,
Because I feared
He'd have so little time
Left to be loved.

He'd lived bravely
His whole life,
The fourth of twelve,
Competing for love

As a child. Then finding
A woman he loved
Who loved him more
Than he could love himself.

Grateful to God for her,
But waging a lifetime war
Against his vulnerability—
Thus limiting intimacy.

She died two years
Before he did, leaving
Him more lost and lonely
Than he could fully admit.

But he began to change.
Yes, he maintained his
Usual routines: dozing;
Woodworking; worshipping

At the same church
In the same Iowa town
He was born and raised in.
His faith sustained him.

But he did start talking
More about his feelings
After she died
Than he ever had—

Which was a blessing:
Him being more open.
It made connecting
With him a bit easier;

Which makes his absence
Harder to bear;
But he was aware
Of the transience

Of all life forms,
Including his body:
The inherent entropy
Countered by creativity—

Which he engaged in
Throughout his life,
As a farmer, carpenter,
And Master Woodworker.

Dad had his wounds
And his flaws, but in his
Life and in his dying, he
Sought to bear witness

To these word of the prophet Isaiah:
"The grass withers, the flower fades;
But the [creating] word of our God
Will stand forever."[1]

For me now, Dad is present and gone,
Gone to his eternal home.
But the Spirit which inhabited
Him for his time lives on.

1. *The Holy Bible (NRSV)*, Isaiah 40:8.

The Weight of Water in Wood

I never knew the
      weight
of water in wood.

I'd never known
      how heavy
wet wood was—

the weight
   of water
in living wood.

I could have known,
    when I heard
      the thump
  of the sawn-off branch
as it hit the ground.

The thump was loud—
   a bump, no bounce,
     dead weight,
      I found out,
   When then I bent down
to pick it up.

Thick as my thigh,
    three feet long;
        it was not easy
            to heft it up.
    For a moment
I was stuck and
struck by its weight.

That momentary pause
    gave added weight
    to my realization
of our common state:

Water is the stuff
    of which we, too,
        are made:
    about sixty percent
of our physical state.

My Dad dried wood
    in a solar drying shed;
        made furniture and clocks
that lasted and lasted.

That's one way that wood
    has an edge on us:
        it can last for years,
whereas we're just dead.

But perhaps we too,
    in a transformed state,
        with the living God
live on to recreate.

Cemetery Walk

On my morning walk I visit the dead,
which calms but also scrambles my head.
In a few years' time I'll lie there too,
or somewhere else when my time comes due.

"Rest in peace," we say, after people die,
which implies that living makes us tired.
This notion of resting soothes and calms me;
but being dead—no thanks, I'm not ready!

In the end, of course, I'll have no control;
but trusting in Spirit can make me whole.
Resting in that is what gives me peace;
surrendering to love without surcease.

Bibliography

Eliade, Mircea. *The Sacred and the Profane: The Nature of Religion.* Translated by Willard R. Trask. San Diego: Harcourt, Brace, Jovanovich, 1957.

Rilke, Rainer Marie. *Letters to a Young Poet.* Translated by Joan M. Burnham. Novato, CA: New World Library, 2000.

Stravers, Jon. *Hawkman Solo* (Compact disc), email: hawk@acegroup.cc, 2019.

The Holy Bible, (New King James Version). Nashville, TN: Thomas Nelson, 1982.

The Holy Bible (New Revised Standard Version). Nashville, TN: Thomas Nelson, 1990.

The Random House Dictionary. New York: Ballantine Books, 1980.